# Believing in You

story by: **Dr. Danielle Hyles**     illustrations by: **Enrico Iskandar**

*iUniverse books may be ordered through booksellers or by contacting:*

*iUniverse*
*1663 Liberty Drive*
*Bloomington, IN 47403*
*www.iuniverse.com*
*844-349-9409*

*Because of the dynamic nature of the Internet, any web addresses or links contained in this book may have changed since publication and may no longer be valid. The views expressed in this work are solely those of the author and do not necessarily reflect the views of the publisher, and the publisher hereby disclaims any responsibility for them.*

*Any people depicted in stock imagery provided by Getty Images are models,*
*and such images are being used for illustrative purposes only.*
*Certain stock imagery © Getty Images.*

*ISBN: 978-1-6632-3085-0 (sc)*
*ISBN: 978-1-6632-3084-3 (e)*

*Library of Congress Control Number: 2021921676*

*Print information available on the last page.*

*iUniverse rev. date: 10/21/2021*

I dedicate this book to my daughter Vivien who I believe in wholeheartedly. She is an example to other children of confidence and courage in herself. To all children, believe in yourself and don't let anyone stop you from believing in your dreams and fulfilling them.

Head up, I believe in you when no one else will.

But more importantly God will.

Chin up dear Vivien.

I have always believed in your ability to be a good friend.

Vivien I believe in your gifting in mathematics.

Look up, God is always with you.

Believe in yourself and your abilities.

Be you.

You are special and loved in every way.

As your mother, from the moment you were born.

I believed in you.

Never forget how much you are loved.

Vivien asked, "What if
I forget to believe in myself?"

Then remember mommy and God
are there surrounding you.

And believe in you and your abilities.

Like your ability to be kind and caring.

Vivien thanks mommy for always believing in her.

Mommy says, "And God too. Goodnight."

Vivien says "Goodnight I love you too."

Vivien and mommy hug.

Mommy gives Vivien a kiss on her forehead.

## About the Author

Dr. Danielle Hyles is a Canadian author with Trinidadian heritage who is currently a school administrator with the Durham Catholic District School Board. She has written a research-based educational leadership book entitled "Bridging the Opportunity Gap" for educators all over the globe. She has also authored several children's books including, "Loving My Working Mom", "Seeds of Belonging", "God's Children Are Math Wizards", "We Can't Stop Now", and "Hugging is My Superpower". "Believing in You" is a book that reminds children to be confident and believe in themselves.

Printed in the United States
by Baker & Taylor Publisher Services